WHAT
THE S.E.L

A Parents Roadmap to Understanding Social and Emotional Learning

Antonio R. Broadnax M. Ed

Published by Success Built on Vision Learning House Publishing.

Printed in the United States of America

CONTENTS

Chapter 1

WHAT IS SOCIAL AND EMOTIONAL LEARNING?

I magine this scenario: Your child is acing their math and science exams, but they struggle to manage their frustration when things don't go their way. Or perhaps they find it challenging to make new friends or communicate effectively with teachers and peers. This is where Social and Emotional Learning (SEL) comes into play.

Understanding the Basics

At its core, SEL is about equipping children with essential life skills that go beyond academic knowledge. It's about nurturing their emotional intelligence, teaching them to understand and manage their emotions, and helping them build healthy relationships.

The Five Core Competencies

SEL revolves around five core competencies:

1. Self-Awareness: This involves recognizing and understanding your own emotions, strengths, and areas for growth. It's the foundation of emotional intelligence.

2. Self-Management: Self-control, impulse management, and stress management fall under this category. It's about handling your emotions effectively and making responsible decisions.

3. Social Awareness: Understanding the emotions, perspectives, and needs of others is crucial for building empathy and developing strong interpersonal skills.

4. Relationship Skills: Healthy relationships are built on effective communication, conflict resolution, and cooperation. These skills are vital in both personal and professional life.

5. Responsible Decision-Making: This competency involves making ethical, safe, and responsible choices. It's about considering the well-being of oneself and others when making decisions.

Why SEL Matters

SEL is not just a buzzword; it's a vital component of your child's development. Here's why it matters:

1. Academic Success: Strong SEL skills can boost academic performance. When children can manage their emotions and work effectively with others, they're better equipped to learn.

2. Emotional Well-being: SEL helps children navigate the ups and downs of life with resilience. It empowers them to

manage stress, build positive self-esteem, and develop a growth mindset.

3. Positive Relationships: SEL fosters healthy relationships with family, peers, and teachers. It enhances communication, empathy, and conflict resolution skills.

4. Life Skills: The competencies learned through SEL are life skills that serve children well into adulthood. They contribute to career success, emotional health, and overall well-being.

Incorporating SEL into Daily Life

SEL isn't confined to the classroom. You can incorporate it into your daily routines and interactions with your child. Start by modeling emotional intelligence, active listening, and empathy. Encourage your child to express their feelings and discuss emotional experiences openly.

As we journey through this book, we'll explore practical strategies, real-life stories, and expert insights to help you embrace SEL and support your child's emotional growth. So, let's dive deeper into the world of SEL and discover how it can enrich your child's life and your relationship with them.

Chapter 2

THE CORE COMPETENCIES OF SEL

I n this chapter, we'll dive into the heart of Social and Emotional Learning (SEL) by exploring its core competencies. These competencies are the building blocks that help children develop into emotionally intelligent individuals who can navigate life's ups and downs effectively.

Self-Awareness

Think of self-awareness as the foundation of SEL. It's about understanding one's own emotions, strengths, and areas where there's room for improvement. It's the ability to recognize when you're feeling happy, sad, frustrated, or anxious, and knowing why you feel that way. When your child is self-aware, they can better manage their emotions and reactions.

Self-Management

Self-management takes self-awareness a step further. It's not just about recognizing emotions; it's about knowing how to handle them. It's the skill of staying calm when faced with a challenge, setting and working towards goals, and practicing self-discipline. This competency helps children learn to regulate their behavior, even in stressful situations.

Social Awareness

Understanding others is a key part of SEL. Social awareness involves recognizing and empathizing with the feelings and perspectives of those around us. It's about being able to "read" emotions in others, which leads to better communication and stronger relationships. When your child is socially aware, they'll find it easier to get along with their peers, teachers, and family members.

Relationship Skills

Relationships are at the core of human interaction. SEL places a strong emphasis on teaching children how to build and maintain healthy relationships. This involves effective communication, cooperation, and conflict resolution. These skills are not only valuable in childhood but are essential throughout life.

Responsible Decision-Making

Lastly, responsible decision-making is a crucial SEL competency. It's about teaching children to make choices that consider both immediate and long-term consequences. It encourages them to think before they act and to consider how their decisions affect themselves and those around them.

These five core competencies work together to create emotionally intelligent individuals who can handle life's challenges, build meaningful relationships, and make responsible choices.

As we continue through this book, we'll delve deeper into each of these competencies, providing practical guidance on how to nurture them in your child's everyday life. So, get ready to discover not only what SEL is but how you, as a parent, can play a pivotal role in helping your child develop these essential life skills.

Chapter 3
WHY SEL MATTERS FOR YOUR CHILD

Welcome to a chapter that uncovers the profound impact of Social and Emotional Learning (SEL) on your child's life. SEL isn't just another educational buzzword; it's a powerful tool that can make a significant difference in your child's well-being and future success.

Building Blocks for Life

Think of SEL as the building blocks upon which your child's life is constructed. These skills are like a secret sauce that helps them thrive in various aspects of life, from school to relationships and even their own mental and emotional well-being.

Academic Success

Surprising as it may sound, SEL plays a vital role in academic success. When kids are equipped with self-awareness and self-management skills, they're better at handling stress and focusing their attention. Imagine the positive impact this can have on their grades and overall learning experience.

Emotional Well-being

SEL is like emotional armor for your child. It helps them understand and manage their emotions, reducing the risk of getting overwhelmed by stress, anxiety, or frustration. It's a toolkit for building resilience, which is invaluable in today's fast-paced world.

Healthy Relationships

The ability to empathize and communicate effectively are two essential skills that SEL nurtures. When your child understands the feelings of others and can express themselves clearly, they're well-prepared to form and maintain positive relationships, both now and in the future.

Preparation for Life Beyond School

Consider SEL as a life-long gift. The skills your child learns through SEL will serve them well beyond their school years. In college, in their career, and in everyday life, these skills are a ticket to success and happiness.

So, as you dive into the world of SEL with your child, remember that you're not just giving them another set of skills; you're providing them with tools that can shape a fulfilling, successful, and emotionally rich life.

In the upcoming chapters, we'll explore practical ways to infuse SEL into your child's daily routine, ensuring that they not only understand its importance but also experience its benefits. So, get ready to embark on this journey of nurturing your child's emotional intelligence and helping them become the best version of themselves.

Chapter 4

HOW SEL BENEFITS SCHOOL SUCCESS

Welcome to the exciting world of Social and Emotional Learning (SEL) and its direct impact on your child's success at school. In this chapter, we'll uncover how SEL skills are like a secret weapon that can boost your child's performance in the classroom and beyond.

Emotional Intelligence and Academic Achievement

Think about it: when your child understands and manages their emotions, they're better equipped to focus on learning. SEL helps create a positive emotional climate, making it easier for kids to engage in class, ask questions, and seek help when needed.

Conflict Resolution and Collaboration

SEL is all about teaching kids how to navigate the social world effectively. When your child can resolve conflicts peacefully, work well with classmates, and communicate clearly with teachers, they're setting themselves up for a more harmonious learning environment.

Critical Thinking and Problem Solving

SEL isn't just about "soft" skills; it's about building critical skills too. When your child learns responsible decision-making through SEL, they become better at evaluating options, considering consequences, and making thoughtful choices in and out of the classroom.

Reducing Stress and Anxiety

School can be stressful, and these emotions can significantly impact academic performance. SEL equips your child with tools to manage stress, reduce anxiety, and maintain a positive outlook, even during exams or when facing challenging assignments.

Building Confidence

Confident kids often excel in school. SEL helps boost self-esteem by encouraging self-awareness and teaching kids to celebrate their strengths. When your child believes in themselves, they're more likely to take on challenges and succeed.

So, as you embark on this journey of exploring SEL with your child, remember that you're not just enhancing their social and emotional skills; you're giving them an advantage in the classroom. SEL isn't separate from academic success; it's intricately woven into it.

In the upcoming chapters, we'll explore practical ways to integrate SEL into your child's daily life and school experience. By doing so, you'll be nurturing not only their academic achievements but also their personal growth. Get ready to witness the positive changes that SEL can bring to your child's school journey.

Chapter 5
PRACTICAL WAYS TO PROMOTE SEL AT HOME

W elcome to a chapter filled with actionable insights on how to bring Social and Emotional Learning (SEL) into your home. Here, we'll explore simple yet effective ways to nurture these essential life skills in your child's everyday life.

1. Open Up Conversations

Start by creating an environment where your child feels comfortable sharing their thoughts and

feelings. Regular conversations about their day, their concerns, and their achievements are a great way to encourage self-expression and emotional awareness.

2. Be a Role Model

Children often learn best by observing. Demonstrate the social and emotional skills you want your child to develop. Show empathy, manage your own emotions positively, and model responsible decision-making in your own life.

3. Emotion Exploration

Help your child identify and label their emotions. Use books, movies, or real-life situations to discuss various emotions and their triggers. This helps them build emotional vocabulary and self-awareness.

4. Mindfulness and Relaxation

Introduce mindfulness and relaxation techniques into your daily routine. Activities like deep breathing exercises, meditation, or even simple stretches can help your child manage stress and improve their self-regulation skills.

5. Encourage Problem Solving

When your child faces challenges or conflicts, guide them through the process of problem-solving. Ask questions like, "What are your options?" or "What could you do differently next time?" This encourages responsible decision-making.

6. Foster Empathy

Encourage your child to consider the feelings of others. Discuss how certain actions might impact someone else's emotions. Reading books or watching movies with strong moral lessons can be a fun way to explore empathy together.

7. Set Realistic Goals

Help your child set achievable goals, both academically and personally. This fosters self-motivation and self-management. Celebrate their successes, no matter how small, to build their self-esteem.

8. Family Rituals

Incorporate SEL into your family rituals. For example, during dinner, you could have a "feelings check-in" where everyone shares how their day went emotionally. This encourages social awareness and communication.

9. Practice Active Listening

When your child talks to you, practice active listening. Give them your full attention, ask questions to understand better, and validate their feelings. This reinforces the importance of open communication.

10. Encourage Play and Creativity

Play is a fantastic way for children to practice SEL skills. Through games, role-playing, and creative activities, they can explore emotions, relationships, and problem-solving in a fun and engaging manner.

Remember, you don't have to implement all of these strategies at once. Choose what feels most natural and enjoyable for your family. The key is consistency. By integrating SEL into your daily life, you're not just teaching these skills; you're creating a nurturing environment where your child can flourish emotionally and socially. So, let's embark on this journey of growth and discovery together!

Chapter 6

SEL IN SCHOOL: HOW PARENTS CAN GET INVOLVED

W elcome to a chapter that explores the dynamic relationship between Social and Emotional Learning (SEL) and your child's school experience. Here, we'll discuss how you, as a parent, can actively participate in and support SEL initiatives within your child's educational journey.

1. Connect with Teachers

Building a strong partnership with your child's teachers is a crucial step. Reach out to them to discuss how SEL is integrated into the curriculum and what you can do at home to reinforce these skills. Communication is key to creating a consistent SEL environment.

2. Attend School Meetings

Participate in parent-teacher conferences and school meetings where SEL initiatives are discussed. This provides an opportunity to gain insights into how SEL is implemented in your child's school and how you can contribute.

3. Advocate for SEL

Don't hesitate to advocate for SEL in your child's school. Share the benefits you've observed from practicing SEL at home, and encourage the school to expand SEL programs and training for teachers.

4. Support SEL Events

Attend SEL events and workshops hosted by the school. These events often provide valuable resources and insights into how you can further support your child's SEL development.

5. Incorporate SEL at Home

Continue practicing SEL skills at home, as discussed in previous chapters. The more your child experiences SEL both at school and at home, the more it will become a natural part of their life.

6. Encourage Peer Relationships

Promote your child's positive peer relationships. Encourage them to invite friends over, engage in group activities, and practice SEL skills in a social context.

7. Monitor Progress

Keep an eye on your child's progress in developing SEL skills. Regularly discuss their experiences and challenges, and offer guidance when needed. Celebrate their successes together.

8. Foster a Growth Mindset

Encourage a growth mindset in your child. Teach them that it's okay to make mistakes, as long as they learn from them. This mindset fosters resilience and a willingness to embrace new challenges.

9. Be Patient

SEL is a journey, not a destination. Be patient with your child and yourself. It's okay to have setbacks; what matters is the progress you make over time.

By actively engaging with your child's school and continuing to nurture SEL skills at home, you're providing a strong foundation for their emotional and social development. Remember, you are a vital part of their SEL journey, and your involvement can make a world of difference in their overall well-being and success in school. So, let's continue this collaborative effort to support your child's growth and happiness!

Chapter 7

COMMON CHALLENGES AND SOLUTIONS

I n this chapter, we'll explore some of the common challenges
parents may encounter while nurturing Social and Emotional
Learning (SEL) in their children and offer practical solutions to
address these issues. Remember, you're not alone in facing
these hurdles; many parents share similar experiences.

1. Resistance or Disinterest

Challenge: Your child may resist or show disinterest in practicing
SEL skills.

Solution: Be patient. Start with activities that interest your child.
Incorporate SEL into their favorite hobbies or games. Show them
how SEL skills can be fun and useful.

2. Time Constraints

Challenge: Busy schedules can make it challenging to find time for SEL activities.

Solution: Integrate SEL into daily routines. Discuss emotions during meals or before bedtime. Use car rides as opportunities for conversations. Small, consistent efforts can go a long way.

3. Age-Related Challenges

Challenge: SEL needs evolve with age, making it challenging to adapt your approach.

Solution: Tailor your strategies to your child's age. Younger children may benefit from storytelling and creative activities, while teenagers may prefer deeper conversations and goal-setting.

4. Balancing Screen Time

Challenge: The digital age poses new challenges for SEL, with screen time potentially replacing face-to-face interactions.

Solution: Monitor screen time and encourage balance. Use technology as a tool for SEL, such as finding emotion-related apps or discussing online interactions and their emotional impact.

5. Peer Influence

Challenge: As children grow, peer influence becomes more significant, potentially impacting their SEL development.

Solution: Encourage positive friendships. Teach your child to apply SEL skills in social situations, helping them navigate peer pressure and conflicts.

6. Limited Resources

Challenge: Some parents may lack access to books or materials on SEL.

Solution: SEL doesn't require fancy resources. Many activities can be done with everyday items or through conversations. Utilize free online resources and local libraries for books and materials.

7. Consistency Challenges

Challenge: Maintaining consistency in practicing SEL can be tough.

Solution: Create a family routine that includes SEL activities. Set reminders or incorporate SEL into existing routines, like dinner discussions or bedtime rituals.

8. Handling Negative Emotions

Challenge: Your child may struggle with managing negative emotions.

Solution: Teach coping strategies, like deep breathing or journaling. Encourage them to express their feelings and offer a supportive, non-judgmental space.

9. Busy Family Life

Challenge: Juggling work, household chores, and other responsibilities can leave little time for SEL.

Solution: Involve the entire family. SEL isn't limited to parent-child interactions; siblings can practice together, making it a family affair.

Remember that challenges are part of the SEL journey. They offer opportunities for growth and learning, both for you as a parent and for your child. Be adaptable and patient, and remember that progress often comes in small, meaningful steps. You're taking an active role in shaping your child's emotional intelligence, and that effort is a valuable investment in their future happiness and success. So, let's face these challenges together, one step at a time!

Chapter 8
YOUR CHILD'S JOURNEY WITH SEL

___

A s we explore the world of Social and Emotional Learning (SEL), it's important to recognize that this journey is uniquely tailored to your child's growth and development. In this chapter, we'll discuss how SEL evolves with age and how you can support your child at every stage.

Foundations in Early Childhood

In the early years, SEL lays its foundations. Young children start to understand basic emotions and how to express them. Activities like reading books about feelings, using simple emotional language, and encouraging sharing and empathy build the groundwork for future emotional intelligence.

Elementary School Years

As children enter elementary school, they become more aware of their own emotions and those of others. This is a prime time to introduce more complex SEL concepts like conflict resolution and effective communication. Role-playing and group activities can be particularly helpful in developing these skills.

Middle School Transition

The middle school years can be a tumultuous time emotionally. SEL plays a critical role in helping children manage the ups and downs of adolescence. Encourage open communication with your child, validate their feelings, and provide a safe space for them to explore their emotions.

High School and Beyond

As your child enters high school and prepares for adulthood, SEL skills become even more crucial. Responsible decision-making and goal-setting take center stage. Discuss long-term goals and the impact of choices with your teenager. Support their autonomy while offering guidance.

Life-Long Learning

Remember that SEL is a life-long journey. Your child's needs and challenges will evolve, and so should your approach. Continue to adapt and refine your SEL strategies as your child grows, and encourage them to take ownership of their emotional well-being.

The Power of Patience

Throughout this journey, patience is your ally. Your child will have successes and setbacks, and that's perfectly normal. Embrace these opportunities for growth and learning, both for you as a parent and for your child.

As you walk alongside your child on their SEL journey, you're providing them with invaluable life skills that will serve them well in every aspect of their life. Be their guiding light, their confidant, and their biggest supporter. Together, you'll embark on a rewarding journey of self-discovery and emotional growth that will shape their future in beautiful ways.

Chapter 9

CASE STUDIES: REAL-LIFE SEL SUCCESS STORIES

I n this chapter, we step into the real world and explore inspiring stories of how Social and Emotional Learning (SEL) has made a significant impact on the lives of children and families. These stories highlight the tangible benefits of nurturing SEL skills and how they can transform young lives.

Sarah's Story: Building Confidence and Resilience

Meet Sarah, a shy and introverted 8-year-old. She often struggled to express herself and was hesitant to make new friends. Her parents decided to incorporate SEL into their daily routine, starting with simple activities like emotional check-ins during dinner.

Over time, Sarah's self-awareness grew. She began to recognize her emotions and found the courage to share them with her family. This newfound confidence spilled over into school, where she started participating more in class discussions.

As Sarah practiced self-management and learned to regulate her emotions, her social interactions improved. She began forming friendships, and her resilience in the face of challenges blossomed. Sarah's journey is a testament to how SEL can empower even the most reserved individuals to thrive socially and emotionally.

James' Story: Overcoming Academic Challenges

James was a bright student, but he struggled with managing his frustration and perfectionism, which often led to emotional outbursts and disrupted learning. His parents and teachers recognized the need to nurture his SEL skills.

Through SEL-focused activities, James learned how to recognize and manage his emotions. He developed self-control and effective problem-solving techniques. These skills not only improved his emotional well-being but also had a direct impact on his academic performance.

With SEL as his tool, James transformed into a more focused and resilient student. He learned that mistakes were opportunities to learn, not reasons to give up. His story illustrates how SEL can be a game-changer in helping children overcome academic challenges and develop a positive attitude toward learning.

Ava's Story: Navigating Middle School

Middle school can be a tumultuous time, and Ava was no exception. She faced peer pressure, friendship issues, and the emotional rollercoaster of adolescence. Her parents and school implemented a comprehensive SEL program that included peer mediation and emotional check-ins.

Ava embraced SEL with enthusiasm. She became an active participant in her school's SEL initiatives and started helping others navigate their own emotional challenges. Her communication skills flourished, and she became a trusted friend and peer mediator.

Ava's story showcases how SEL can empower young adolescents to not only navigate the emotional ups and downs of middle school but also become leaders and mentors, positively influencing their peers.

These real-life stories highlight the transformative power of SEL. They show that with dedication, patience, and the right support, children can develop the emotional intelligence and resilience needed to succeed academically, build healthy relationships, and face life's challenges with confidence. SEL isn't just an educational concept; it's a tool that can shape the future of our children in profoundly meaningful ways.

Chapter 10

FREQUENTLY ASKED QUESTIONS

I n this chapter, we'll explore some of the most commonly asked questions about Social and Emotional Learning (SEL). These questions reflect the curiosity and concerns of parents like you who are eager to understand and support their child's SEL journey.

1. What's the Difference Between SEL and Traditional Education?

Traditional education primarily focuses on academic knowledge, while SEL complements it by emphasizing essential life skills such as emotional intelligence, self-awareness, and relationship-building. Both are important, and when combined, they create a well-rounded education.

2. How Can I Tell if My Child Needs More SEL Support?

Look for signs of emotional struggles, difficulty in managing relationships, or academic challenges linked to emotional well-being. Open communication with your child can help uncover their needs. Remember, every child is unique, so the signs may vary.

3. Can SEL Help with Bullying Issues?

Yes, SEL can be a powerful tool in addressing bullying. It equips children with empathy, conflict resolution, and communication skills, making them less likely to engage in bullying behavior and better able to handle it if they're targeted.

4. What Age Is Suitable to Start Teaching SEL Skills?

SEL can start as early as preschool with basic emotion recognition and empathy-building activities. It evolves with age, becoming more complex as children mature. It's never too late to begin teaching SEL, and it can be adapted for different age groups.

5. How Can I Encourage My Teenager to Open Up About Their Emotions?

Create a safe and non-judgmental space for your teenager to express themselves. Respect their boundaries and offer support without pressure. Sometimes, indirect conversations like discussing a movie character's emotions can open doors for discussion.

6. What Role Should Schools Play in SEL, and How Can I Support It?

Schools play a crucial role in teaching SEL skills. You can support their efforts by staying involved, attending meetings, advocating for SEL programs, and reinforcing SEL at home. Collaborate with teachers to ensure consistency.

7. Is There a Right Way to Implement SEL at Home?

The "right" way to implement SEL at home is what works best for your family. Start with open conversations, actively listen to your child, and incorporate SEL into daily routines. Experiment with different activities and adjust based on your child's needs and interests.

8. Can SEL Help with My Child's Academic Performance?

Yes, SEL can have a positive impact on academic performance. By improving emotional regulation, self-awareness, and focus, children are better equipped to engage in learning and perform well in school.

9. How Can I Balance SEL with Other Parenting Priorities?

Balancing parenting priorities can be challenging. Incorporate SEL into existing routines and activities, making it a natural part of family life. Remember that even small, consistent efforts can make a big difference over time.

10. What Resources Are Available for Learning More About SEL?

There are many books, websites, and organizations dedicated to SEL. Look for reputable sources that offer guidance, activities, and research on SEL. Additionally, your child's school may have resources and programs in place.

These are just a few of the common questions parents have about SEL. The key is to be open to learning, adapt to your child's needs, and remember that nurturing emotional intelligence is a journey that can be incredibly rewarding for both you and your child.

Chapter 11

SUPPORTING YOUR CHILD'S EMOTIONAL WELL-BEING

I n this chapter, we'll explore essential strategies and insights for parents to support their child's emotional well-being. Nurturing emotional health is a lifelong gift you can give your child, and it begins with understanding and support.

1. Be an Active Listener

One of the most powerful ways to support your child's emotional well-being is by being an active and empathetic listener. Encourage your child to express their feelings, thoughts, and concerns openly. Create a safe and non-judgmental space where they feel heard and understood.

2. Validate Their Emotions

It's important to validate your child's emotions, even if you don't fully understand or agree with them. Let them know that their feelings are legitimate and that it's okay to feel the way they do. This validation can help your child develop emotional resilience.

3. Teach Emotional Regulation

Help your child learn how to manage their emotions in healthy ways. Teach them techniques like deep breathing, mindfulness, or taking a break when they're overwhelmed. These skills are invaluable in handling life's challenges.

4. Encourage Expression Through Art and Play

Children often find it easier to express their emotions through art, play, or creative activities. Provide them with outlets for self-expression, such as drawing, painting, or imaginative play. These activities can help them process and communicate their feelings.

5. Maintain Consistent Routines

Consistent daily routines can provide a sense of security and stability for your child. Predictable schedules help reduce anxiety and create a safe environment for emotional growth.

6. Promote Healthy Habits

A well-balanced diet, regular physical activity, and sufficient sleep are crucial for emotional well-being. Encourage healthy habits that contribute to your child's overall health, both physically and emotionally.

7. Monitor Screen Time

Excessive screen time, especially on social media, can impact your child's emotional well-being. Keep an eye on their online activities and promote responsible internet use. Encourage face-to-face social interactions and outdoor play.

8. Seek Professional Help When Needed

If you notice persistent emotional issues or behavioral changes in your child, consider seeking the help of a mental health professional. Early intervention can be crucial in addressing and managing emotional challenges.

9. Model Healthy Emotional Expression

Children learn by example. Model healthy emotional expression by demonstrating how to manage your own feelings and resolve conflicts positively. Your actions speak louder than words.

10. Celebrate Their Strengths

Acknowledge and celebrate your child's strengths and achievements. Encourage them to explore their interests and passions. A strong sense of self-esteem can boost emotional well-being.

Supporting your child's emotional well-being is an ongoing process that requires patience, understanding, and a deep commitment to their happiness. By actively fostering emotional health, you empower your child to navigate life's ups and downs with resilience and confidence, setting the stage for a bright and emotionally fulfilling future.

Chapter 12

SEL AND DIGITAL AGE CHALLENGES

I n this chapter, we'll explore the unique challenges presented by the digital age and how Social and Emotional Learning (SEL) can play a vital role in helping children navigate this increasingly complex digital landscape.

Understanding the Digital Age

The digital age has ushered in unprecedented opportunities for learning, connection, and entertainment. However, it also presents challenges, particularly for the emotional well-being of children.

1. Digital Citizenship

Teach your child the importance of responsible digital citizenship. Discuss the impact of online behavior on others and the consequences of cyberbullying. Encourage empathy and kindness in their online interactions.

2. Balancing Screen Time

Finding a healthy balance between screen time and offline activities is crucial. Set reasonable limits on screen time and encourage your child to engage in physical, creative, and social activities outside of screens.

3. Managing Screen-Related Stress

Excessive screen time can lead to stress and anxiety. Teach your child to recognize when they need a break from screens and provide alternative stress-reduction activities, like outdoor play or reading.

4. Addressing Cyberbullying and Online Harassment

Discuss the importance of reporting any instances of cyberbullying or online harassment to a trusted adult or authority figure. Make sure your child knows they can turn to you for support if they ever experience such situations.

5. Online Privacy and Safety

Educate your child about online privacy and the potential risks associated with sharing personal information. Encourage them to use strong, unique passwords and to be cautious about the information they share online.

6. The Impact of Social Media

Discuss the impact of social media on self-esteem and self-worth. Encourage your child to curate their online experience by following positive influences and taking breaks from social media when needed.

7. Building Healthy Online Relationships

Teach your child to build healthy and positive online relationships. Emphasize the importance of respectful communication and encourage them to report any online interactions that make them uncomfortable.

8. Digital Detox and Mindfulness

Introduce your child to the concept of digital detox and mindfulness. Teach them the importance of unplugging from screens regularly and engaging in activities that promote emotional well-being.

9. Model Healthy Tech Use

As a parent, model healthy technology use. Be mindful of your own screen time and demonstrate responsible digital citizenship to your child.

10. Open Communication

Maintain open and non-judgmental communication with your child about their online experiences. Encourage them to come to you with questions or concerns related to their digital activities.

Navigating the digital age is a shared journey for both parents and children. By incorporating SEL principles into discussions about digital usage, you can help your child develop the emotional intelligence and resilience needed to thrive in the digital world while maintaining their emotional well-being.

Chapter 13

PREPARING FOR TRANSITIONS

T ransitions are a natural part of life, and they can evoke a wide range of emotions in both children and parents. In this chapter, we'll explore how Social and Emotional Learning (SEL) can help prepare your child for various life transitions.

Understanding Transitions

Transitions can be both exciting and challenging for children. Whether it's starting school, changing schools, moving to a new home, or any other significant change, SEL can provide valuable tools to navigate these shifts.

1. Open Communication

Maintaining open and honest communication with your child is essential during transitions. Encourage them to express their feelings and concerns. Listen actively, validate their emotions, and provide reassurance.

2. Emotion Recognition

Help your child identify and understand their emotions related to the upcoming transition. Use stories, role-play, or art to explore how they're feeling. This self-awareness can empower them to manage their emotions effectively.

3. Building Resilience

Transitions often come with uncertainties and challenges. Teach your child resilience skills, such as problem-solving and adaptability, to help them face these changes with confidence.

4. Social Skills

SEL can enhance your child's social skills, making it easier for them to connect with new peers and adapt to new environments. Encourage them to practice active listening, empathy, and effective communication.

5. Positive Self-Talk

Help your child develop positive self-talk and a growth mindset. Teach them to view transitions as opportunities for growth and learning rather than as intimidating changes.

6. Maintain Routines

During transitions, maintaining some familiar routines can provide stability and comfort. Continue with established bedtime rituals or family traditions to anchor your child in a sense of normalcy.

7. Visit New Environments

If possible, visit the new school, neighborhood, or place before the actual transition. Familiarity can ease anxiety and make the new environment feel less intimidating.

8. Seek Support

Transitions can be challenging for parents too. Don't hesitate to seek support from other parents, school counselors, or community resources. Sharing your experiences and concerns can provide valuable insights and emotional support.

9. Celebrate Achievements

Celebrate your child's achievements and milestones related to the transition. Whether it's the first day of school or making new friends, acknowledging their successes boosts their confidence.

10. Be Patient

Transitions take time. It's normal for your child to have a period of adjustment. Be patient and offer consistent support as they navigate the changes.

Remember that transitions are opportunities for growth and development. By integrating SEL principles into your approach, you can help your child not only survive but thrive during times of change. Building their emotional intelligence and resilience will equip them with the skills they need to face life's transitions with grace and confidence.

Chapter 14

CONCLUSION AND NEXT STEPS

A s we come to the end of this journey through Social and Emotional Learning (SEL), it's important to reflect on what we've learned and consider the next steps in nurturing your child's emotional well-being.

Reflecting on the SEL Journey

Throughout this book, we've explored the significance of SEL in your child's life. We've discussed the foundational principles of emotional intelligence, the practical strategies to support SEL, and the unique challenges of the digital age. You've gained insights into fostering resilience, preparing for transitions, and the lifelong journey of SEL.

Celebrating Progress

Take a moment to celebrate the progress you've made in embracing SEL as a parent. You've taken proactive steps to equip your child with essential life skills that will serve them well in every aspect of their life. Your dedication to their emotional well-being is commendable.

Next Steps in Your SEL Journey

The journey of SEL is ongoing. Here are some next steps to consider:

1. Continual Learning: Keep exploring SEL resources and stay informed about the latest developments in the field. Knowledge is a powerful tool in nurturing emotional intelligence.

2. Consistency: Maintain the SEL practices you've incorporated into your daily life. Consistency helps reinforce the skills your child is developing.

3. Collaboration: Work closely with your child's school or educational institution to support SEL programs. Collaboration between home and school enhances the impact of SEL.

4. Expand Your Network: Connect with other parents who are also on the SEL journey. Share experiences and learn from one another's insights and challenges.

5. Encourage Leadership: Encourage your child to take on leadership roles in SEL initiatives at school or in your community. Empowering them to share their knowledge fosters a deeper understanding of SEL.

6. Stay Adaptable: As your child grows, their SEL needs will evolve. Be ready to adapt your approach and explore new strategies that align with their age and development.

7. Self-Care: Remember that your own well-being is crucial. Practicing self-care and managing your own emotions will enable you to be the best support for your child.

8. Share Your Journey: Consider sharing your experiences and knowledge with other parents or caregivers who may benefit from your insights.

The journey of nurturing your child's emotional intelligence is a gift that will continue to unfold throughout their life. Embrace it with enthusiasm and the understanding that you are shaping not only their future but also the future of our communities and society at large.

Thank you for embarking on this journey with us. Your commitment to your child's emotional well-being is a remarkable testament to your love and dedication as a parent. Here's to a future filled with emotionally intelligent, resilient, and compassionate individuals who will make a positive impact on the world.

"Unlock the power of Social and Emotional Learning (SEL) to guide your child towards a brighter, emotionally intelligent future. In 'Nurturing Hearts: A Parent's Guide to Social and Emotional Learning,' we embark on a heartfelt journey into the world of SEL, where academic excellence meets emotional well-being.

Discover the transformative impact of SEL on your child's life, from boosting academic success to nurturing resilient, empathetic individuals ready to face life's challenges. With real-life stories, practical strategies, and expert insights, this book empowers parents to be champions of their child's emotional growth.

Join us on this enriching adventure, as we celebrate the immense potential within every child's heart."

www.ingramcontent.com/pod-product-compliance
Lightning Source LLC
Chambersburg PA
CBHW071243090426
42736CB00014B/3198